"Somewhere in New England one will find Purgatory Road. I associate Charles Coe with this region of America as much as I do W.E.B. DuBois. In his latest collection there are many poems of mindfulness and daily rituals. Coe writes about aging as well as close encounters with white people that are lessons passed down from fathers to sons. His haiku are snapshots. There are lines in *Purgatory Road* that are as memorable as one's heart beat. "A squirrel is dragging a large slice of cheese pizza up a tree..." Lines like this will stop a reader somewhere between heaven and hell. Coe writes like a man with polished wings, flying above it all while watching the high and low tides of life."
— **E. Ethelbert Miller**, co-editor, *Poet Lore* magazine and founder/ director of the Ascension Poetry Reading Series

"In *Purgatory Road*, Charles Coe has given us a contemporary urban Spoon River Anthology. Empathy, fellow-feeling, Caritas, Metta, call it what you will, Coe brings his whole joyful heart and his considerable craft to the portrayal of both the living and the dead ("an endless parade of ghosts.") Time and again these poems not only remark on the distances between us but invite us to close them; they even sometimes suggest how. Coe speaks of — and with — a kind of neighborliness that moves from curiosity to attention, from puzzlement and mirth to warmth and appreciation. This is the work we need now."
— **Richard Hoffman**, author of *People Once Real*

"Charles Coe is a classic storyteller who crafts anecdotes, parables, and poems of fable-like quality—in a language as forthright as it is unfussy. Often beginning in the quotidian, Coe pitches us into greater realms, and through time's portals in striking ways. A number of *Purgatory Road's* poems are stamped with the author›s inimitable wit; some bear the gift of the surprising journey. All, however, reflect his talent as a noteworthy raconteur."
— **Danielle Legros Georges**, author of *The Dear Remote Nearness of You*

Charles Coe

NEW AND SELECTED WORKS

Leapfrog Press
New York and London

Published in 2024 by
Leapfrog Press Inc.
www.leapfrogpress.com

Printed in the United States of America

Distributed in the United States by
Consortium Book Sales and Distribution
St. Paul, Minnesota 55114
www.cbsd.com

Back cover author photo © Gordon Webster
Design and Typesetting: James Shannon

First Edition

ISBN: 978-1-948585-69-972

This book is dedicated to my parents, Connie and Edith Coe, and to my sister Carol, all of whom live on in my memory...

Some of the poems in this collection have appeared in the following publications: *Ibbetson Street Magazine, Poesis, Solstice Magazine, Meat for Tea: The Valley Review, and Spectrum Magazine.*

Table of Contents

From *All Sins Forgiven: Poems for my Parents* (2013)

From *Memento Mori* (2019)

From *Purgatory Road* (2023)

New Works (2024)

Prelude

Before we begin, may I ask you a question?
Would it bother you if at some point
I forgot to remember the illusion that we
are made of solid matter? That we instead
consist of atoms and electrical charges,
are ninety-nine percent empty space?

Would it bother you to look through
my suddenly spectral form and see
the backrest of this chair?

It wouldn't be intentional, a parlor trick.
It's just that when I think about broken children
lying in the rubble of bombed-out buildings
I sometimes find it difficult to remain tied to this world.

So if I seem to fade please don't judge or be alarmed.
Just hold out your hand. We can touch, palm-to-palm,
to keep ourselves connected to this terrible and beautiful place,
remind us we are made of the same stuff as the stars.

Walkabout

not ashamed to admit,
don't run as fast as I once did
now when I see that bus pull out
I just shake my head and watch it go.

not ashamed to admit
not much hair left on my head
but the summer breeze feels fine
and I just grab a hat when it gets cold.

I'm wearing one now
on this frost-tipped night
breathing stars in and out again
walking along the borderland

carrying the moon as a secret charm
against the old regrets that try
to hang themselves around my neck
like a string of pearls.

Role Reversal

A frail, elderly man walks slowly into the clinic,
one hand on his cane, the other
on the on the arm of a middle-aged woman
who guides him across the room
to a chair, on the seat of which
sits an empty plastic cup someone left behind.

He stares a long moment as it has
some significance he can't quite grasp
before the woman, without disturbing
his grip on her arm picks it up, tosses it
into a trash can, eases him into the chair
and sits in the one beside him.

His eyes drift around the room
and he seems unsettled
as if in an unfamiliar land where the signs
and signals are unreadable.

She takes out a tablet and turns it on
to show something on the screen
that seems to relax him, even brings a little smile.

As I watch I suddenly imagine them
walking down a sidewalk,
him young and strong
her a giggling toddler
taking three steps to his one,
when he stops to lift her in the air
holding her up to the sky,
as if giving thanks.

This Tomato

Tonight's dinner is a single tomato,
a massive heirloom, ruby red,
wrinkled and irregularly shaped
local, perfectly ripe, sliced thick,
sprinkled with salt.

I never bother with tomatoes
in the off season, those billiard balls
shipped cross country, picked green
gassed to turn them red.
And when the good tomatoes are done,
my tongue's attention turns elsewhere.

When I was young and waved goodbye
to friends who'd packed their lives into
cars and headed down the road,
I always assumed I'd see them again someday.
Some I never did, and never will.

I hope I'm here to greet next year's crop
but now I take nothing for granted.
Tonight's tomato, this tomato,
is an exercise in the ephemeral,
a juicy, vine-ripened reminder
of time's blinking eye.

Refrigerator Magnet Triptych

you chant to worship the goddess milk
the ache of languid beauty on your tongue

ask the diamond moon
she will never lie

may you dream of a delirious purple sky

Mulligan

At first glance the toddler in the baby carriage seems sleepy but a closer look makes it clear the child isn't sleepy, but bored. And it's an exquisite boredom, world-weary and nonchalant, as if all the diversions and entertainments life has to offer have been tried and found wanting, tossed aside like empty candy wrappers.

You might meet the child's eyes in passing and offer a smile but the little one is unamused, expression unchanged as if to say, "This incarnation fails to meet my most minimum standards. When I get back to Central that dispatcher's getting a piece of my mind."

Because

Because the manufacture and sale of bombs is an extremely profitable business

Because those who profit from the production of bombs will never experience their effects

Because at the end of day, people who make bombs can go home to hug their children

Because bombs are designed to take things apart not put things together

Because bombs are deployed without risk to those who deploy them

Because bombs whisper "collateral damage" as they embrace their targets

Because the light of an exploding bomb is brighter than the sun

Because the words of politicians are written on the bombs in blood

Because at the moment of detonation, the fulfillment of their destiny, we cannot know whether bombs feel satisfaction or sorrow

Because the dogs that search for broken bodies buried beneath the rubble later dream strange and restless dreams

Mulberries

One day near the end of summer vacation
when all the easily picked berries had been plundered
a few buddies and I climbed the tallest mulberry tree
in Military Park on a dare, to the highest branches
that would support our weight, and lying back
on sturdy limbs, lounging like young lords,
reached out to pluck those darkest berries
beyond the reach of earthbound peasants,
our only competition the indignant birds
who complained at the intrusion before flying off.

With machine-like efficiency we dispatched
those berries bursting with juice that dyed our lips
and tongues and teeth purple and ran down our chins.
Eating our fill, beyond our fill, we finally slowed,
leaning back on our thrones in the sky.

Down on the ground the world carried on
in the usual way. There was the distant cry of a baby
in a carriage, the rumble of a truck, like muted thunder.

And all the while, creeping up like a slow-moving fog,
the inevitability of sixth grade, of starched nuns
and math homework, and one more step toward distant,
unimaginable adulthood. We had no words
for any of this. We just felt it in our muscles, our bones.

As golden light filtered through the leaves
and late afternoon melted into early evening.
we knew our mothers stood on porches and back stoops,
waiting to call us to the suppers for which we now had no room.

The hard branches had begun to punish our backs
and the rough bark chafe our skin, so on some silent signal,
like birds changing course midflight, we began the descent,
coming down more carefully than we'd climbed,
returning reluctantly to the ordinary world.

Grace Notes: A Fairy Tale

Imagine, if you will, a smoky little night club,
on a hot summer night, many years ago,
when the emcee climbs a little wooden stage
and steps to the microphone:

*"Ladies and gentlemen, we have a special treat
tonight. Won't you please put your hands together
for Brooklyn's own all-girl do wop ensemble...
"The Pirouettes!"*

Five young women are bathed in cat calls
and wolf whistles as they step into the spotlight,
stand quietly until the room becomes silent
and then begin to sing, softly, gathered around
the single microphone.

As some song of love found, or maybe lost,
floats through the cigarette smoke,
it quickens the blood of these young lovers,
and as the alto leans in to take her solo,
the room is silent.

When the song ends
and the last notes fade away,
in the stillness before the room
erupts in thunderous applause
all the would-be James Deans,
and all the girlfriends with their
Annette Funicello hairdos, look into
each others' eyes, and at least for the moment,
their dreams don't seem so foolish after all.

Sanctified

When The Blind Boys of Alabama kick into high gear a hole is ripped in the fabric of the universe through which you will tumble to find yourself in a storefront Baptist church in Selma, Alabama, with no air conditioning, on the hottest day of the summer, at Sunday service, where shouts pouring from the open windows are heard a block away and Sister Hattie, whose magnificent hat is the love child of Mt. Kilimanjaro and The Sydney Opera House, is fanning herself with one hand and with the other dabbing at the "glow" on her cheek with a lace hanky.

Turn it Up

A gritty convenience store in old Dudley Station, now Nubian Square, in Boston's mostly black Roxbury neighborhood, winter of '83, years before gentrification, when most blocks had at least a few boarded-up brownstones and you kept your eyes open when you walked around at night. The store is a late-night demilitarized zone for hookers and cops and drug dealers and junkies and potheads and other miscellaneous alien lifeforms, a place where five bucks buys a "nickel bag," an under-the-counter tiny yellow envelope with a few joints worth of seedy, mediocre pot.

The guy at the cash register looks like an out-of-shape college linebacker, with gold tooth and coal-black shaved head. When "Little Red Corvette" comes on the radio he jacks up the volume to sing along, captured by the music of a skinny, androgynous kid he probably would have beaten up back in high school.

At the bridge, cash register guy loses his mind. Head back, shoulders wagging, wailing like a wounded ox while a grinning white cop waits patiently in line to pay for his Slim Jim and Coke.

An Invitation to Duke

Dear Mr. Ellington,
I would like to invite you to dinner
at a time convenient for you
to take temporary leave
of your current digs
so you can tell me
what it was like
to sit late at night in a hotel room
in Paris or London or Rome
smoking cigars, drinking bourbon
and writing charts and in the morning
hearing them played at rehearsal
by some of the finest musicians on Earth.

If you care to join me
I will offer your favorites:
a steak smothered in onions
with a double portion of fried potatoes,
sliced tomatoes, and a giant lobster,
and over apple pie à la mode
we can chuckle about the time
some snob asked what you thought
of Ray Charles playing country music
expecting you to criticize but instead
you said, "There are only two kinds
of music: Good music and the other kind."

Girl Talk

An elderly couple in a coffee shop. The woman's talking with, or rather at the man in quiet, pissed-off rapid-fire Russian. His hands are wrapped around a paper cup, into which he stares as if wishing he could crawl inside. Whatever battle there might have been is clearly over. He's simply listening now as she lays out the terms of surrender.

She stops for breath as an employee pushes a broom near their table, a young woman with skin so dark it looks almost blue, and long cornrows covered with beads that rattle when she moves her head. A queen reincarnate from an ancient African kingdom, now amusing herself sweeping up napkins and straw wrappers. She stops and says to the woman, "I love your lipstick," a deep ruby red.

The woman switches to English and shares intel about brand and shade. "I love your beads," she says, then smiles and strokes her own hair—wispy and snow-white. "Maybe I should get some."

Friends

Two little girls are in the yard of the house next door where one of them lives, squatting like farmers in a rice paddy, examining with scholarly seriousness an early spring flower poking through the grass.

They're always together, the only girls on my one-block dead-end. Sometimes they kick a ball around. Others they do elaborate chalk drawings in the street, moving to the sidewalk when the rare car turns onto the block to park.

Someone I know in her seventies recently attended the funeral of a lifelong friend. They met her first day of second grade at the new school she attended after a family move. She was sitting alone for lunch when a classmate sat to say hello. The seed of that moment sprouted into a lifelong friendship, through marriages, divorces, births, and deaths. When they lived apart the distance between them was a rubber band that stretched across a continent but never broke, and when she heard of her friend's death she crossed that continent to be with her one final time.

Relationships are often born of circumstance and as circumstances change those bonds might weaken and sometimes break. I look at these little girls drawing on the asphalt in their own created world and wonder what their future holds. Of course, there's no way to know. Maybe someday when they move on to adult life the days spent at play will become fond memories and occasional holiday cards.

Or maybe on some distant day, one of them will drive slowly in that line behind a long black car, stand on a rainy morning in a field of green grass, and watching the other being lowered into the ground.

Let's Not Talk About It

A Texas public history schoolbook once described enslaved Africans as "black immigrants."

Imagine if you will, these "immigrants" preparing for the journey to the New World. Throughout West Central Africa excited villagers gather around cooking fires, ebon faces shining in the flickering flames, preparing celebratory feasts as their fellow tribesmen ready for the journey across the big water to their new lives.

Those joining the exodus are unbinding from possessions they have to leave behind. ("Here, Brother...take my plow." "Sister, this loom I made with my own hands, it is yours.")

At departure the shore is crowded with those shouting good wishes as the immigrants climb onto the sturdy ships that will carry them across the rolling waters.

On days when the sea was calm, they take turns standing at the ships railing breathing in the clean, salty air, staring at the horizon, longing for sight of this new land where they will create the new lives of which they'd dreamed for so very long.

For Ruby Bridges

In the Norman Rockwell painting "Ruby Bridges The Problem We All Live With," you are being escorted into the segregated school by federal marshals. We see four of them in the frame, two walking ahead, two behind, but we don't see their faces. You are the focus of the piece.

A thrown tomato is smashed on the wall behind you. You walk straight ahead, past the red guts dripping down and piled on the sidewalk, past the faint ghost of "NIGGER" painted on the wall someone tried, with limited success, to scrub away.

Ruby, what can we possibly say about you? What words can describe this six-year-old child, armed with only a notebook and ruler, walking resolutely past that pack of jabbering hyenas, past the woman who every day threatened to poison you, past the woman who every day waved before your face a black doll in a coffin?

The lead marshal said you never cried once during that nightmare year. What can we possibly say about you, brave as any astronaut climbing into a tin can to be launched into the airless void?

Privilege

When I was a child one day a white man in a Cadillac
ran a red light and t-boned our family's station wagon.
Nobody was hurt but both cars were totaled.

He was dead drunk. When police came he could hardly stand.
They loaded him into the back of a squad car and spirited him away
without taking a statement from my father.

His insurance paid to replace our car but he was never charged
with drunk driving. I told my father I didn't think it was fair,
he could have killed us all.

Father looked at me a long moment,
then turned back to the mirror without answering,
razor slowly plowing the field of shaving cream.

To the Mother of a Black Son

He doesn't like you hugging him in public.
Sometimes the music he listens to makes you sad.
"Where is the tenderness," you wonder, but say nothing.

This man child, taller each time he rises from his bed,
who grows stronger by the day, whose veins flow
with blood that busies itself building muscle and bone,
is without realizing it already laying, brick by brick,
the path that will lead him away to some unknown future.

Some mornings when he's off to school and you tell him
to be careful he shrugs. If you try to speak of this world's
cold truth, about how quickly clouds can darken the sky,
he might say he "already knows."

But he doesn't know. And as you watch him walk
out the door every morning you pray the phone
never rings with the news you dread.

haiku for george floyd

that final moment
when you called out for "mama"
did birds go silent?

Nocturnal Admissions

Late at night, and I reluctantly shed the cocoon
of blankets, rise once again to perform that task
so familiar to men of a certain age, and afterwards
look for a moment in the bathroom mirror
at the battalion of wrinkles whose comrades
wait patiently to join their ranks.

I look at my hair, what's left of it,
mostly white as a sheet of typing paper,
then shut off the light and go back to bed
to burrow once more beneath the covers.

But as sometimes happens, sleep has climbed
out the window, dropped quietly to the grass
and padded off barefoot into the night.

At times like this one's shortcomings and failures
and disappointments return to take their bows,
projected on the ceiling, images on parade.
I nod to each member of the troupe
and accept each judgement in turn.
Some debts I can never repay.
Others will never be repaid to me.

But even though the list of things I thought I knew
grows ever smaller, and the tang of ancient griefs
still lingers on my tongue, I realize that I've made peace
with my past and to my surprise, sleep returns. I awake
to sun shining through the window and hear a mockingbird
declare itself master of the universe.

Now that my nocturnal ghosts have faded once more
into memory and mist, I will rise to face this new day
that stretches out before me like a ribbon of new highway.

Blues for Mister Glasper

This is how Mr. Glasper
my next door neighbor
spent his Saturday afternoons
in Indianapolis, Indiana,
during the summer of 1967:

He'd unfold a card table covered
with yellow plaid contact paper
and set it up in the middle of his scrubby
back yard. On the table he'd place
a dinky little record player–the kind
that only handled 45s–and plug it into a long line
of skinny, patched-together extension cords
that snaked through the crabgrass
and draped over the back porch rail.

Then he'd pile on a load of records,
plant his long, skinny body in a lawn chair,
and drift away on the Delta blues,
on songs of love gone wrong and pockets
full of empty. He'd sit, legs crossed,
eyes closed, in a feathered golf hat,
nodding to the beat, while voices rubbed raw by cotton dust
and homemade whiskey floated through his yard.

I could have stuck my fuzzy head over the fence
and asked what he was listening to,
but I didn't have no time for the blues. Man,
the world was on the move! Reverend King
was pulling black people out of the mud.
Sidney Poitier was getting *rich*
making movies, and acting
like a man! Not like some
bug-eyed darky, flapping his arms
and yellin' about some ghost.

So I didn't want to hear no twangy-twang,
old-timey, nappy-headed, watermelon-chewing music
played by refugees from a minstrel show.
I wanted Sam Cooke and Marvin Gaye, smooth and sharp
and all dressed up for Saturday night.
I couldn't hear the echoes of the Delta
in those brothers' songs.

I didn't realize then that blue is a primary color.

On Working with Slate Roofing Shingles

Though their gray, bland faces seem
to reveal nothing
slate shingles will tell you
how they want to be handled.
They don't like being bent
or tossed around.

Try lifing a small pile of slate shingles
and you'll soon discover
there is no such thing
as a small pile
of slate shingles.
So take your time.
They will sit
patient as stones
awaiting your pleasure.

There was a summer
of backaches and swinging hammers
when I helped take down
a leaky old slate roof

Of the hundreds of shingles we handled
someone noticed that one had
writing on the back.

Looking closely we saw
two names scratched in,
and below,
a date:
August 11, 1917.

The shingles we lowered to earth
with block and tackle
and heartfelt curses
those two men
a lifetime ago
had put up nail by nail.

Passing that shingle around
we grew quiet
as if noticing for the first time
the blue sky
the fine ache of young muscles
the coolness of sweat
drying in the summer breeze.

In the House of Echoes

When her brother Albert finally died,
my mother was relieved
the tubes and wires
that had kept him tied so painfully to Earth
could finally be disconnected.

He hadn't let his sisters visit him those last few months;
my mother called it "old-fashioned masculine pride,"
but toward the end, when he was beyond knowing
who sat beside his bed, his four sisters
took their turns in the quiet room,
holding a hand as gray and light as dried grass.

At Christmas time, a few weeks later,
my mother and her five remaining siblings
sat around a dinner table where nine children
once argued and laughed
and lobbied for their parents' attention.
In a house grown quiet with years they talked
about their mother–round-faced and gentle,
always filling the house with the smell of baked hams
and apple pies–and of their father, quiet and serious,
his ox-blood leather easy chair and rack of Meerschaum pipes
sitting undisturbed for the thirty-five years since he died.

They told stories about Albert, and his brothers
Charles and Lawrence,
also gone, and they sipped egg nog
and nibbled ham sandwiches.
Finally, when the conversation lagged,
someone started singing Christmas carols,
and echoes filled the dark old house.

In the silence that followed the last carol,
a silence neither pained nor awkward,
merely thoughtful,
as each sat with his or her own memories,
my mother whispered softly,
to no one in particular,
"Three down, six to go."

Get On Up!

Can anybody else here say
that in the summer of 1967,
when they were fourteen years old,
their mama took them to a James Brown concert?

Did you walk alongside her
through the gates of
a minor-league ballpark
on a hot, cloudless Indiana night
when the moon shone like a spotlight
on the rough wooden stage?

Was anybody else here sittin' beside their mama
on those hard benches
When James's band, the Famous Flames,
came out to lay down
a red carpet of funk
and the announcer whipped that crowd
like a bowl of black cream
'til the Godfather of Soul finally skated onstage
like a waterbug,
tellin' everybody 'bout his brand-new bag?

If your mama yelled like everybody else,
then let it now be told!
Let everybody know how
she clapped her hands raw
as James flew back and forth across the stage,
with sweat and grease from his conked-up hair
pouring down the front of his ruffled shirt,
purple satin jacket ripped off and tossed aside.
Let everybody know how she stomped her feet
when he grabbed that mic like a dog grabs a bone,
fell to one knee,
and begged for "just one more chance,

baby, baby please,"

And then, when he finally rose, shaking and spent,
and someone tossed a robe over his sloping shoulders,
and helped him trudge offstage,
did your mama scream when he suddenly froze
in his tracks–as if struck by the Holy Ghost–pulled away
from his helper, tossed that robe aside,
and ran back into the spotlight?

And is there anybody else
whose mama popped out of her seat
like a piece of toast
when the band scratched out the opening licks
of "Say it Loud, I'm Black and I'm Proud"?
And did she scream herself hoarse shouting out the chorus,
while James, wearing a coast-to-coast grin,
held his mic aloft to gather in the music of the crowd?

Was your mama there? Then stand up and testify!
Get on up! And Shout it out!

My Sister Read to Me

Nestled in my sister's lap
while she read a picture book
or fairy tale
I would trace trails
across the pages
that carried me to
other worlds.

I don't know how or when
My sister's path
carried her away from
sun and sky
to some strange world
light never reaches

where needles and spoons
and burning candles
are the nodding faithful's
machinery of prayer.

For a long time
she never read at all
just lay abed
behind closed door
television glowing in the
darkened room.

But something has changed
Now she emerges from her cave,
like a bear in spring
hungry, a bit confused
wincing at the unaccustomed light
shielding eyes that discourage questions
yet reveal all.

Rise up,
Daughter of Cleopatra,
who challenged mighty Rome

Daughter of Sojourner Truth,
whose white-hot gaze pierced the heart

Daughter of Artemis, goddess of the hunt,
arrows flying straight and true.

Rise up,
Daughter of ancient women warriors.

My sister,
you read to me,
and opened doors
you could not
walk through yourself.

If What You Say is So

If what you say is so
that the world's heart
is cracked and crumbling
I must make ready
for the coming round
of gray days.
I will stand before cracked mirrors
practicing dyspeptic scowls to flash at babies
when their mothers' backs are turned.
When children play outside my window
I will shout down curses
like those dry old men who hate life
because it reminds them of death.

Will you then be satisfied?
When my eyes are covered
with that thin, tough film
that lets light neither in
nor out?

We can sit together then
in a cozy little room
and wiggle our toes before the fire
and sip our tea
and laugh at the fools
who still believe
that a life can be saved
by one hand
reaching for another.

Surplus Populations

Once, you needed us.
Walking silently along the furrowed ground
you watched our dark, hunched shapes
blend with the earth.

When you heard our voices
drift across the fields
you told yourself our songs
were the songs of happy children.

But now
there is little left to plant
little left to carry.
We look into the bright
faces of your new machines and know
that we are no longer needed.

So
where will we go?
What will we do?

We gather, restless.
on hot city streets

the ancient spirits
of our tribes
dance before us,
shake their dry rattles,
chant the old chants,

but we cannot hear them.

Invisible to us
in this strange new land
they seek familiar holy places
and finding none
can only wander endlessly
among towering temples
glass and steel.

Meditation on the Loss of Empire

There comes a day
when after years at the top
the old bull elk can't meet
the young bull's charge
and shambles off into the dark woods.

The upstart
bloody face raised to the sky
sings his victory song
never sees his own fate
mirrored in the old bull's eyes.

Somewhere
at this very moment
hands begin to shake
that never shook before
sweat covers
a newly wrinkled brow
and chills creep quietly
into some heart
that never before
knew fear or doubt.

The game never changes—
only the players.
Today the young bull
is master of the world
but his bones will be the toys
of some child
yet unborn.

Over the Hump

1. This morning,
   while you walked to work,
   the wind,
   for the first time, ever,
   was at your back.

2. At lunch
   you pondered your tomato,
   and that moment
   within the sun-warmed earth
   when a seed said
       yes.

Opening the Refrigerator Door

Opening the refrigerator door,
I peer inside-in search of a miracle:
three slices of mushroom pizza,
or some leftover beef lo mein?
But the empty shelves recite
that simple law of physics
the mind knows,
but the stomach forgets:

"Nothing can be taken from a refrigerator that
was not first placed inside it."

But what if someday, behind
that door, something's there that wasn't there before?
Some patient morsel,
sitting in that cold white light?
Would I accept the gift, open-faced
and trusting as a child,
or would I slowly back away,
remembering that when the apple comes,
the snake must follow?

News from the Front

I have nothing interesting, nothing amusing to relate.

The shower leaked. A plumber came. He was unsmiling
and wore a tattoo. He replaced old fixtures with new.
I shall never see the old ones again.

The telephone rang. No one was there.

There is nothing to say. A package arrived
in the mail. Inside the package was a letter
promising eternal salvation in exchange
for a small donation. There was also
a plastic statuette of the Virgin Mary,
which I have given a prominent place
on my bedroom dresser.

I await her instructions.

A paper bag, filled with sand, sits in the trunk
of my car. The sand is for traction in the snow.
There is no snow, yet the bag remains.

There is no news. I returned two library books.
The books were several days overdue,
but there was no fine. The librarian said
there was a "grace" period for overdue books
before a fine was collected.

Grace is that few minutes we are allotted
each morning before being charged for the entire day.

Nothing has happened. The vegetables at the supermarket
are wilted. Automatic sprinklers were installed recently
in hopes that shoppers would equate moisture
with freshness. Sometimes the sprinklers
actuate themselves while the shoppers
are leaning over to inspect the produce.
When this happens, the shoppers become wet
and curse the produce.

I have nothing to report. No one is taking a shower.
The telephone does not ring. No snow falls.
The Virgin gathers dust.

The vegetables are silent.

Yo, Poets!

Here's a list of never-nevers:

Never read a poem
in a room
with a television set
(even if the set is off).

Never try to soften
a hardened heart
with a poem slipped
under a door
or left on a desk
or stuck to the 'fridge
with a plastic banana magnet.

Never read a poem to someone
who has to take a serious piss
or is expecting
an Important Telephone Call.

Never write a poem
when you could be making love
or eating a dish
of strawberry ice cream.

But most important,
when committing an act of poetry,
never be a slave to rules.

Picnic on the Moon

Lacus Veris, Aristarcus, Mirna Arideus ...
those names roll so smoothly off the tongue.

The Moon sounds like the perfect picnic spot–
a great place to bask in the warm solar breeze
and take a break from the earthly roar and rumble.

Yesterday a bomb went off beside a school bus.
Some child's blood-stained notebook lay
across a seat–one day's journal entry
in some ancient, endless war.

Right now, someone is cleaning his gun
in preparation for the evening news. His eyes
are shooting stars, spinning off into darkness.

Mare Imbrium, Oceanus Procellarum, Gassendi Crater...

Let's catch the Lunar shuttle–
spread a blanket on the soft gray ash
share our homemade pickles
with the Man in the Moon
and see just how far
a champagne cork can fly
in the airless lunar sky.

Last night I watched my laundry orbit the dryer
and wondered which shirts had been sewn
by children locked inside some windowless room.

Serenitatis Basin, Mare Crisium, Mare Tranquillitatus...

Don't be sad when we climb into the shuttle
for the trip home.
For we each will carry back

a cool and quiet place within ourselves
and the next time
we wake to the sound of gunfire
we can gaze into the night sky
and remember when

we nibbled grapes at the crater's edge
and watched the children
kick up clouds of lunar dust, their faces
smeared red–not with blood–but ketchup
and raspberry jam
as they romped beneath a blue-green earth
that glittered like a fragile and precious jewel
across the trackless miles of space.

For Rosa Parks

It might have been easier
to let the moment pass.

It might have been easier
to rise with a sigh
from the creaking seat
trudge past those
pale, uneventful faces
and take your customary place.

Afterwards,
before walking the rest
of the way home
you might have stood
for a silent moment
in the wash of exhaust
to watch that bus
lumber off into the twilight.

But something happened ...

Maybe your aching feet
and the driver's tone of voice
together tipped some hidden scales,

and the slow anger
that had grown for years
was finally called to birth.

Later,
when asked to explain,
you simply said:

"I was tired."

The Alchemist
for Etheridge Knight

The Alchemist would sit before his fire
muttering and chuckling to himself
and sipping dark potions
that were forbidden to the children.

His scarred brown face
glowed crimson in the flames
and when he spoke
the words rolled slowly off his tongue
like great stones
that gathered speed as they tumbled
through the listener's mind.

Those who came to sit
brought pieces of their souls
to toss into the fire.
Sparks would fly
flames would crackle
like chicken bones
in a hungry dog's mouth
and smoky fingers
climbed the sky
to caress the distant moon.

The Alchemist bore wounds
from wars of many sorts
and a thousand years of suffering
softened his bones
but still he'd smile
rub his stubbly chin
and lean to whisper
his warm-breathed secret in your ear:

While demons prowl the dark
just beyond the fire's glow
the poet stirs
a pot of words
and changes lead to gold.

On the #1 Bus

The very large man
who squeezed me against
the window of the # 1 bus
at 7:15 on a Monday morning
turned to ask
if I wanted to see his pet rattlesnake.
"It's very friendly," he claimed.
"It only bit the mailman twice."
"Thanks anyway," I said,
"but I only look at snakes on Tuesdays and Thursdays."
This seemed to satisfy him.
A bit later he asked, "You know what would really
liven up this bus? If ten thousand
killer bees suddenly poured through the door
and swarmed up the center aisle."
"Hmmm," I replied. He did have a point.

At the end of the day
on the return ride
a young woman hopped up
to leave the bus
and her wallet
with keys dangling
fell to the seat.
I grabbed it and tapped her on the shoulder.
"Excuse me miss, did you drop this?"
She looked wary for a moment
then her face opened like a flower.
I tucked her smile in my pocket
to warm the walk home.

Long Live the Queen
for Ella Fitzgerald

Fourth of July, 1958
at a backyard barbecue
my face buried in a plate of
hot dogs, baked beans and coleslaw,

when a voice sliced
through the grease and smoke–
a voice as hot as grandma's barbecue sauce
as cool as lemonade on ice–
a voice that changed everything.

A singer with a strong sense of rhythm
is said to "keep good time."
Ella, you didn't just keep time
You grabbed him by the ankles,
turned him upside down,
shook the change from his pockets
flipped him back onto his feet
slapped him on the ass
and sent him on his dazed
and dizzy way
cheek smeared with scarlet lipstick.

When you got it goin', eyes shut tight,
sweat rollin' down your face,
your sideman wore the same amazed expression
the apostles exchanged that time
Jesus called Lazarus back for an encore.

Five hundred years from now
on a mining ship light-years in space
some young jazz cat will be lying in bed
listening to you sing *Moonlight in Vermont*,
someone who's never breathed real air
or walked through a forest in autumn
but hearing your voice
will reach out
with eyes closed
to grab a handful of fallen maple leaves,
and breathe their faint perfume.

When Charlie Mingus Played His Bass

When Charlie Mingus played his bass
burnished wood glowed like black ice.

Eighth notes and sixteenth notes
dashed, naked,
through the smoke-filled room–
playing hide and seek–
and kissed each other
on the lips.

When Charlie Mingus played his bass
rivers danced with the moon–
left muddy footprints all along their banks.

Spirits of the trees recognized
their brother's song
and hummed along
deep in ancient forests where no light
ever shone–except at night.

You could hear
your heartbeat keeping time
and stray cats yowling at the moon
and dust motes floating in Pharaoh's tomb

when Charlie Mingus played his bass.

She Awakens

This poem was written to commemorate
the twentieth anniversary of Boston's Casa Myrna Vazquez,
a shelter for battered women and their families.

She awakens
late in the night

throws aside
the dream-soaked sheets
and sits upright in bed.

In this unfamiliar room,
the shadows are strangers
And night speaks a foreign tongue.

Her ears long for
the slow drip, drip, of her kitchen faucet
for the hum and click of the metal box
outside her bedroom window
that changed the traffic light
from red, to green, to yellow, to red
endlessly reciting its one unchanging prayer.

She rises
and steps into the darkened hallway.
In the home she left behind,
she could find the bathroom in the dark
while half asleep.

But now, she walks slowly
her careful feet search their way
across the creaking floorboards.

She fumbles
for the light switch
and squints
in the flickering fluorescent glow.
Her bruised face, framed in the mirror
reminds her where she is,
and why.

She remembers him
standing over her, yelling:
"You're lucky I put up with you
without me, you wouldn't be nothin'
nothin'
nothin'..."

She remembers
the squeal of tires
as he sped away.

She remembers rising from the floor
comforting her crying child
reaching for the packed suitcase
hidden beneath the bed
carefully unfolding the
well-worn piece of paper
with the telephone number
she had already memorized.

She remembers sitting in the cab,
as streets lights floated past.
She turned to look one last time
as the house grew smaller–
a distant receding shore.

She stares now into the bathroom mirror
her bare feet against cold tile
touches her face with shaking hands
as tears wash away the life she has left behind.

She could not tell you how
she broke the bonds of fear and pain.
She could not tell you why one seed opens
While another lies stillborn in the dark earth,
but she knows that a journey has begun
from which there is
no turning back.

She turns out the light.
It is easier now to find her way in this house.
The shadows have become her guides
and the room no longer unfamiliar;
entering, she hears the whispered
welcomes of those who have gone before.

She walks
softly to her sleeping daughter's bed
to watch the small
blanket-covered mound
rise and fall
in the full moon's light.

Her swollen lips
speak a silent vow:
"Never again."
Never again
will her daughter hear
the song of fist against face
that bitter melody
each generation
teaches the next.

And late in the night
in this quiet house
with one hand resting
on her sleeping daughter's brow

she awakens.

Possibility

The new snow covers everything.
This morning, the world was bathed
in that sharp-edged light
that comes in winter
after a storm blows through.
Outside my window, on the street below,
a small child, an electric-blue bundle
lets go of an adult's hand
to charge headfirst into a towering snowdrift.
When a snowplow comes
to shove aside the early morning quiet
the child stares, transfixed, as it rumbles past.

The new snow covers everything.
It covers cars that can be found only
by remembering where they were parked,
and digging like archeologists
seeking clues to some ancient civilization.
People who pass each other without speaking
each morning on the way to work
are now laughing and shoveling together,
good-natured butts of Mother Nature's joke.

The new snow covers everything.
It covers dogshit and cigarette butts.
It covers used condoms and losing lottery tickets
and under this impossibly blue sky
on what seems like the very first morning of the world
the city is an old whore in a white wedding dress
clutching, like a fistful of flowers,
the idea that in spite of everything
we know to be true
about the world and ourselves
we might, somehow,
begin again.

all sins forgiven

poems for my parents

charles coe

DNA

The young woman on the bus
wearing headphones
has a mole on her neck.

Perhaps the same mole
in the same place
on some ancient ancestor
itched with sweat as she
crawled on hands and knees
through the king's garden,
back bent, pulling weeds.

I know someone whose husband
died a month after their baby's birth.
Years later, she had to turn away
when her teenaged son brushed
the hair from his girlfriend's
face with exactly the same gesture
as the father he had never known.

Some mysteries are greater
than the birth of stars;
that sound you hear the moment
before sleep is not the wind,
but your own flesh, in a timeless,
whispered conversation with itself.

Evidence

On Christmas morning, the empty plate sat on the dining room table near the Christmas tree. The night before, I had carefully placed a half dozen peanut butter cookies in a semicircle that followed the contour of the plate. Now all that remained were a few crumbs, the missing cookies evidence of Santa's visit, along with the presents piled under the tree.

My sister Carol and I had taken over the kitchen. Carol, four years older and wiser, played along as I tried to figure out Santa's favorite cookie. I was about to settle on chocolate chip when Father glanced up from the newspaper. "I read somewhere Santa's got a thing for peanut butter cookies," he said. "The chunky kind." Only by coincidence did peanut butter happen to be Father's cookie of choice.

Late that night Father wrapped the presents, his rough laborer's hands so comically unsuited to the task, taking the occasional break for milk and another of Santa's cookies.

A Meeting of Minds

One day when my first-grade class was learning to write, Sister Edna took the pencil from my left hand, put it in my right, and told me to keep it there.

When I told Mother that night she said nothing, but the next morning she got on the school bus. After morning mass, as children filed into class, she pulled Sister Edna aside and asked, "Sister, did you tell my son he can't write with his left hand?"

Sister Edna replied she had indeed, went on to explain that left-handed children "have problems developing verbal skills" and smear ink on the page when their hands drag over what they've written. Mother heard her out, then said quietly, "Sister, my son is left-handed."

The two women stared at each other a long moment, like convicts on the yard, until finally Sister Edna nodded.

To this day, I remain left-handed.

A Symphony of Crickets

I owned one suit as a child—a reddish-brown, wide-wale corduroy number with red and gold paisley fake silk lining—that one Christmas, Mother intentionally purchased two sizes too big. ("You'll grow into it," she replied to my whined objections.)

It was made of cheap, heavy fabric that bent only grudgingly at the elbows and knees; I was Frankenstein's monster, stomping stiff-legged through the forest, chased by torch-wielding villagers and their determined bloodhounds. And the pants rubbed with humiliating ferocity; I was a walking symphony of crickets.

I wore my suit the day in eighth grade I took two buses, alone, to hear Isaac Stern perform with the Indianapolis Symphony. I was studying violin, and spent hours in the library, headphones on, listening to his records. I'd saved enough from my paper route to buy a ticket, and when I got to the hall I climbed to my seat high in back of the balcony, one brown face awash in a sea of white, in my little cheap suit, listening to the maestro, my crickets and I, transfixed and silent.

How My Father Learned to Cook

Because of tomatoes in a neighbor's garden,
my father learned to cook. Because of late summer
home-grown Indiana tomatoes, drooping on the vine,
my father learned to cook. Imagine him at twelve leaning
over the fence of the neighbor's garden, curious but shy,
and the neighbor pointing to the open gate.
Imagine Father digging in the soil, caught in the rhythm
of the gardener's dance
and later handing his surprised mother
the overstuffed paper bag.

A pretty story, but it never happened; here's what did:

Because of tomatoes in a neighbor's garden,
my father learned to cook. But not because he
admired them, or helped weed or pick them; he and
his buddies stole them to throw at houses and stray
cats and passing cars: crimes reported
to their parents by various adult informants.

His mother, raising him alone, had done her best
to play the father's role, though she found it hard to
discipline her rambunctious son. But the day a neighbor
called with news of the tomato escapade, she devised a
punishment diabolical in its simplicity. She marched him
to the kitchen, perched him on a stool, told
him he was grounded and made him watch her cook.
What a cruel fate for a young buccaneer who longed to be
out kicking trashcans and shooting birds with BB guns.
Confined to a kitchen and forced to watch women's work.
So impossible to know which of them was more surprised
when his mood shifted from sullen anger to curiosity, when he started asking,

66

"How you know that meat's done without cuttin' it?" or
"How can you tell that bread's ready to bake?"
Until one day she said, "Go wash your hands.
I'll show you how to knead the dough."

So, because of tomatoes in a neighbor's garden,
my father learned to cook. Because of late summer,
home-grown Indiana tomatoes, sun warmed, drooping
on the vine, nestled like baseballs in the palm
of a young boy's hand.

Day Labor

To feed his young family during the lean years, my father would stand on a certain street corner in the early morning winter dark to wait for the day labor van. The men gathered there would wave their arms and stomp in place as if warding off evil spirits. When the van appeared the boss would look them over, point to some, and ignore the others. The chosen ones would climb inside and doze in their seats, or stare out the windows as the lights of the sleeping city floated past.

They were a mixed lot: black and white, some stories just beginning, others closer to the end. At the city market they would spend the day loading produce from California and Florida and Mexico onto trucks, their breath steaming in the chill warehouse air, oblivious to the bright labels on the crates—fantasy images of sun-drenched worlds they would never know.

Steel

For thirty-five years my father worked at the Chevrolet plant,
a place filled with giant presses that could stamp out the hood
for a pickup truck in a single stroke. Danger hung in the air like
perfume; everywhere were signs marking the number of days
without an accident, but everyone knew that the count, no matter
how high, sooner or later went to zero. As it did the time someone
let his attention wander and a stamper took his arm above the
elbow with a cut as clean as a surgical saw. "Respect steel," Father
once told me. "Mess around with steel and steel wins every time."

Steel took that worker's arm, but it also sent him disability checks
for life. It allowed my father, a man with only a high school
education, to buy a house, feed and clothe a wife and two children
and send those children to private school. And it was giant rolls
of steel, riding steel rails day and night, my father's factory turned
into the shiny dream machines that filled the roads in the summer
of American Empire.

Sleep Cycles

As a young woman, my mother had a recurring nightmare;
she was alone in a horse-drawn carriage with no driver that
raced toward a cliff and plunged over the side. She always
woke a moment before the carriage crashed to the ground.

beneath an unforgiving sun
no guiding hand to slow their pace
foam-flecked and wild, the horses run.

as once again they set upon
this changeless and eternal race
beneath an unforgiving sun.

spurred by a dread of what's to come
that Morpheus cannot erase
foam-flecked and wild, the horses run.

the spectral carriage thunders on
although in passing leaves no trace
beneath an unforgiving sun.

a contest that cannot be won
yet for eternity they face
foam-flecked and wild, the horses run.

a fate that cannot be undone
trapped in this arid, barren place
beneath an unforgiving sun
foam-flecked and wild, the horses run.

Riverside Park

Years ago, on the north side of Indianapolis
was an amusement park where "colored"
people couldn't go. There were no "whites only"
signs; it was understood that the city's Negroes
would teach their children how to live inside
the dotted lines.

One Saturday morning, in an act of teen rebellion,
my mother and her girlfriends decided it wasn't
fair that only white kids could ride a merry-go-round.
Without telling their parents they got on the
northside bus to Riverside Park.

But when they got off, and walked up the driveway
to the gate, the white guard stared in astonished
rage—shouted, "Where you niggers think you goin'?
You know you can't come in here! Go on. Git!"

And then as if these words weren't enough, he
bent to scrape up gravel to fling at them, like a
farmer shooing crows from his cornfield.
Terrified, humiliated, the girls turned to run,
and left childhood lying
in the driveway of Riverside Park.

Imagine them on the bus ride home, faces streaked
with salt, and ringing in their ears the voice of a man
one might be tempted to dismiss as a cartoon cop
policing carousels and cotton candy,
but one who would have easily fit in with certain
distant colleagues who at that moment, after a long day
loading their pale, emaciated charges into the hungry
ovens, were sitting to family supper, and in
the morning would calmly brush from their cars
the fine gray ash that drifted day and night
from silent, lead-colored skies.

Joan of Arc

Mother, you would not have laid down your sword for just
anyone. Dripping with the blood of unsuccessful suitors, it was
a talisman you waved to frighten off the faint of heart. Those
who failed to heed the warning found their heads on stakes along
the road, fields sowed with salt, mothers weeping at their sons'
foolish, fatal pride.

A warrior bested once in battle was twice as vigilant. The price
of having let down your guard was the small girl child who
dashed along in your angry wake, a pony-tailed reminder of the
faithlessness of men. Later, when another man came along with
his patient, soft-spoken way you instinctively recognized the
threat and prepared for battle.

But instead of plunging the blade into his unprotected heart, to
everyone's surprise, not least of all your own, you hung your
sword upon the wall.

No surrender comes without regrets; sometimes in the passing
years you'd cast a jaundiced eye his way; your glance would shift
to the wall, and your weapon's patient gleam; your palm would
long to caress once the rough leather grip. Yet for all those years
you kept your head, and Father, his.

Fort Bliss, El Paso, Texas: August 1951

The milk-white sun gazes down like the eye
of some implacable lizard.

In the photograph, you squint in brand-new
uniform, shirt too large, as if yanked off a shelf
and tossed your way after some bored corporal's
cursory glance. The cap clings to your new buzz cut
at the proper angle, but Father, you look like exactly
what you are: a boy playing soldier.

Some barracks buddy, forever anonymous,
snaps the shutter; you trade places,
later, send pictures home to mothers who
will lie awake, because they know that
fire and steel love the taste of young flesh.

Fortress

Mother never socialized with the neighbors. She was always polite when they crossed paths, but kept her distance and never visited or invited visits.

Only once do I remember a neighbor ever ringing our bell. Mrs. Glaspar, the church lady next door, had just made a load of peach pies and in the spirit of Christian charity had come to give our family one. Mother set the pie on the kitchen counter, thanked her and chatted awhile but didn't ask her in. Mrs. Glaspar seemed to understand, and after a few more pleasantries took her leave.

While Mother watched her walk across the yard, I watched the pie. It was a beautiful shade of brown, a little darker at the fluted edges. Golden nectar had bubbled up through slits in the crust and burned slightly, like caramel. It was still warm; I leaned over and washed my face in the scent of ripe peaches, cinnamon and nutmeg.

Mother waited until Mrs. Glaspar was back in her house, then picked up the pie and tossed it into the garbage. "I don't know how clean that woman keeps her kitchen," she said, and without another word returned to the never-ending task of cleaning the already spotless house, the fortress that no one but family was ever allowed to enter.

Marksmanship

My mother would sometimes toss off
comments that might seem innocuous
to observers, but for the intended target
were fraught with meaning, darts dipped
in neurotoxin that caused instant paralysis.
She couldn't help herself, the way a tongue
can't resist a loose tooth.

I know now what I didn't know then,
That cruelty is the child of fear,
But I don't know, will never know,
what faceless demons guided her aim
as each black-feathered shaft struck home.

My Mother Cut My Hair

The routine never varied:
Saturday mornings in the kitchen
the chair with the vinyl seat
that stuck to my legs when I wore shorts
towel draped over my shoulders
newspapers spread across the linoleum.

I never felt so much distance between us
as in those seemingly intimate moments.
We seldom spoke; the only sounds
were the whisper and click of scissors,
the endless murmur of the television
drifting in from the living room.

As she stood behind me
dressed in motherhood's ill-fitting robe
I wonder what messages she read
in the hair that settled at her feet
like snow from some private winter?

Colossus

Father, when I was a little boy, you filled
the sky, a brown giant whose footsteps
shook the Earth. When you put your hands
on a thing that needed moving,
that thing would move.

Summertime I'd tag along while you
painted houses, lie in thick grass and watch
you grab that heavy wooden ladder,
wrap your hands around the side rails,
set your feet, arms bulging in your shirt
as that ladder floated free from the Earth.

Now your walk is slow and stooped,
its careful rhythm marked by your house
shoes' whispering slide across the kitchen floor,
and you seldom lift anything heavier than a coffeepot.

Last fall you leaned a ladder against the house,
climbed up to clean the gutters, but when you
tried to climb down the ladder started sliding,
your legs too weak to hold it steady.
You sat thumping on the roof with a hammer
waiting to be rescued.

"If no one had been home," you said months later,
"I'd probably still be up there." So like you to
joke at your own expense. But I wonder: what
were you really thinking, as you tapped that
patient Morse code on the asphalt roof?

Last Christmas I saw a snapshot
that I thought at first was you,
but it was me; the glasses, the thinning
salt-and-pepper hair, the beard now
whiter than yours.

So strange: In my mind I'm still twenty,
not this middle-aged man captured
by the camera's unapologetic eye. I am
learning, as you have learned,
that the flesh has its own agenda.

And I want to know: what was it really like
up on the roof? What did you see?
On that warm October afternoon,
looking down at young boys zooming back
and forth on final shirt-sleeved bike
rides of the season, at squirrels gathering
nuts for the winter, under the neighbor dog's
watchful eye, and in the distance, a nearly
empty bus, small as a child's toy,
making its stately way up Sixteenth Street
under a sun that dipped slowly in the western sky?

For the Young Surgeon Who Told My Mother She Needed a Triple Bypass

When you walked into the room, you seemed not much older than our paperboy in your oversized white coat, and black-framed glasses that kept slipping down your nose.

You barely took time to introduce yourself, then like a mechanic describing an engine job, explained how a circular saw would be used to slice Mother's breastbone in half. After veins from her arms and legs had been harvested to replace the clogged ones now feeding her heart, her ribs and breastbone would be pushed back into place and wired together. Of course there is some risk, you said, but it was a "routine procedure."

When you glanced up from your clipboard to ask if she had questions, did you see the iron gate slam shut across her face? Once she declined your little saw, chose instead the long slow slide, she was no longer your concern. Did that frail old woman, covered with goose bumps in a cold examination room, ever cross your mind again? Or had you already forgotten her that night in some restaurant as you cut your steak, the red river flowing on the white china plate?

This Little Gray House

Mother, all those years of living like
a fist in this little gray house
must have taken their toll.

The shades drawn, always,
The puzzled sunlight wondering
why it had been forever banished
from these rooms.

As a child, I tiptoed through the
eternal twilight, antennae twitching
at your ever-shifting moods,
too young to understand that
refuge can be prison.

At your funeral, your sister
Touched my arm and said,
"Your mother should never have
had children. But she did the best she could."

Now I stand in this silent, empty house
clutching the list of ancient grievances
that crumbles to dust in my hands.

Teaching My Imaginary Son to Fish

Never take fishing too seriously. Find a shade tree by the creek bank to lean against on a sunny day with a mild breeze blowing. Toss your line into the water and set aside, for a while, the cares of the day. Never move too fast; in fact, try to move as little as possible. And remember: sometimes your best days fishing will be the ones you go home empty-handed.

These are lessons my father taught me; not in words, but in the way he'd whistle while unraveling a tangled line, or just laugh when some big catfish slipped the hook. I am the end of my father's line, with no one but you to teach those things I am only now beginning to understand. And I struggle with his final lesson, the mere fact of his absence, an idea that wriggles in my grasp, like a worm I can't seem to thread onto the hook.

The Geology of Grief

Deep inside the earth, an irresistible force
cracks the mantle of rock that separates
crust from core. Shock waves swim to the
surface to shatter ancient mountain ranges
like piles of brittle bones.

Eventually, orange sky fades to gray,
ash and smoke subside and a bitter tang settles
on the tongue. We climb from the wreckage,
toss our useless maps aside and explore
the new landscape on feet forevermore
denied the illusion of solid ground.

All Sins Forgiven

And now the empty rooms, the pictures
gathering dust in a hall, the closets full of
clothes, the old hand-wound clock, sitting
silent on the bedroom dresser.

And now the featureless plane, a line stretching
beyond the horizon of those who wait to sign
a massive ledger, to record the words said and
unsaid, the acts of commission and omission,
the grand and petty failures.

Each writer when done passes the pen to the
one behind, moves off to join a giant circle. Finally,
when all have written, the book is set afire and in
the vast silence a single voice intones:

Blessed be those who were bound by chains
they could not break.

Blessed be those who wrapped the same chains
around others trusted to their care.

Blessed be all who took pen in hand to sign
The Book of Regrets,
all sins forgiven,

awakened from the dream of life.

Christmas Night, 1957

Grandma's house was packed with family and friends,
orbiting a dining room table jammed with cakes, pies and
cookies, a clove-studded, honey-glazed ham, a bronze turkey
slightly smaller than a baby pterodactyl, and at the center,
the star of the show: a gigantic crystal bowl that appeared
but once a year, with a half-gallon chunk of vanilla ice cream
floating in a lake of Grandma's eggnog.

It had always been Grandpa's job to stir in a fifth of Kentucky
bourbon. But for the first time this ritual was performed by one
of his sons. Uncle Roy, perhaps, or Uncle Albert, I don't remember
which. But I remember Grandpa's oxblood leather easy chair, empty
this year for the first time, keeping a silent watch on the proceedings.
At five I had no yardstick to measure the hole that chair created in
my mother's childhood home; I was too busy weaving through the
forest of grown-up legs for another piece of pie.

Finally, with the children overtired and sugar crazed, our coats and
hats were gathered and the exodus began. All night the spiked nog
had been off limits to my sister and me, but the taste we were allowed
just before leaving made us easier to load into the car. On the ride
home, while I dozed in the backseat, our station wagon was the world,
warm as a womb, the faithful engine's tireless hum, and drifting from the
front, a lullaby: the murmur of our parents' voices.

Poems

Memento Mori

Charles Coe

Inventory
for the poets of Norfolk Correctional Institution

As a child I tried to keep track of certain things:
cracks in the sidewalk between the bus stop and school,
names of streets between the bridge and our family's house,
toy soldiers lined up on a shelf

Now the list of things I've lost, or forgotten,
or thrown away, at times seems longer
than the list of what remains.
Sometimes this feeling visits uninvited, late at night,
when every breath is a footstep
measuring the miles till dawn.

But this gray morning as I walked across the yard,
the sun suddenly shoved through the clouds
to warm my face, and later I was graced
by a small kindness from an unexpected source.

This is not the life I would have chosen.
But I will try to keep an open hand
for the gifts it spreads each day across my path,
like Easter eggs hidden in the grass.

For the Ancient Boston Bar with Neon Shamrocks in the Windows, Recently Departed

Years ago one rainy afternoon
I wandered into the bar
in search of a pay phone.

Scattered in the gloom
a dozen pairs of eyes
as cold and hard as Irish granite
glanced up and settled
on my dark skin.

I know that in the proper circumstance
anyone there might have been delighted
to crack my skull.

Even so, I've seen enough
of what I thought was mine slip away
that when I pass their old haunt
with its shiny new façade
and the flock of brightly plumed
young revelers whose mating calls
fill the night, I can't help but feel a twinge.

Loss makes brothers of us all.

Sermon

Driving in the rain late one night and fiddling with the radio, I stumbled across a Haitian Creole station with a preacher in mid sermon, voice pouring from the speakers in a full-throated, rhythmic roar, extolling the glories of salvation.

Perhaps at that very moment some lost soul was pulling to the side of the road, rain pouring down his windshield, surrendering grief and fear and guilt in a torrent of tears, forehead against the steering wheel, while in the little studio the preacher kept calling listeners to 'Jezi Kri'– Jesus Christ, eyes shut tight, shirt collar open, tie loose, drops of saliva baptizing the microphone.

And behind him on the wall, the hands of a clock traveling their endless orbit . . . marking the minutes of this mortal life.

The Dance Hall at Porter Square

Near the entrance to the Porter Square subway stop
is a small tree-shaded concrete plaza, off to the side
where street people congregate
and where yesterday I heard an old boombox
call out that it was "Time to get together, and love
one another right now," and saw a shirtless young man
in a grimy Red Sox cap hold out his hand
to a young woman who at first
only smiled and shook her head
as if embarrassed to be asked to dance
in such a place, or because life on the street
had already taught that joy is not to be trusted,
or maybe, because she'd just never learned to dance
in that old-fashioned way,
where two people hold each other
as he was offering to hold her now
an offer that seemed courtly, not seductive,
letting her come to him if she chose
which she did, finally,
like a shy maiden at a country fair
to take the offered hand,
and I was tempted to stop and watch
but some flowers bruise when touched
so I just kept walking, while they fumbled for,
then found, their common rhythm and a flock
of pigeons fluttered their wings in applause.

Taking Down the Tree

A massive tree, dead and leafless,
surrounded by men in hard hats and goggles,
gathered like wolves around an ancient bull elk
feeding chunks of the carcass into a voracious chipper,
cars squeezing slowly past, drivers staring at the spectacle.

An old man walking his dog has stopped to watch.
He leans against a fence, arms folded, face unreadable,
while the dog sniffs the air and looks on, curious,
at the ghosts of a billion leaves that float in a slow circle
drifting on the cool morning breeze.

Yardwork

On the grounds of a Brattle Street
Tory Roy mansion two men are working,
short and squat, broad-chested, bow-legged,
so alike they could be brothers,
Aztec warriors reincarnate
who in a distant past marched
shoulder-to-shoulder terrorizing the southern plains
clad in quilted cotton armor, wooden helmets festooned
with the symbols of the fierce jaguar or eagle clan.

Now one lifts a large plant from the bed of a pick-up truck,
corded muscles flexing as he lowers the heavy pot onto a cart.

The other, with arms that once wielded the
Maquahuitl, the massive wooden sword lined
with razor-sharp obsidian that conquistadors
claimed could behead a horse with a single stroke,
spreads mulch beneath a hydrangea bush
his rake moving in a slow meditation
his ancient face quiet and still.

Sonnet for the Young Woman Who Offered Me Her Seat on the Train

Your smile illuminates the gloomy morn
As sunlight warms a chilly mountain lake
Before me sits a beauty not yet born
When decades trailed already in my wake
You stir as if to rise and yield your place
But I return your smile and shake my head
While hoping in the moment that my face
Will show no hint of all my thoughts unsaid
I could have sung your mother lullabies
Though still a young man lingers in my heart
Who once delighted in a young girls sighs
The time has passed for him to play that part
He read his lines upon a satin stage
But as they will the years have turned the page

Ceremony

In ancient times when I was young and strong
and paid the rent by painting houses
a certain diner was a favorite breakfast spot
for those in the building trades.

But one morning we arrived to find the doors
wide open with no kitchen crew in sight,
just a gang of laborers, pallbearers
in work boots, loading benches and coolers
into a truck while we dazed regulars
huddled in the cold.

Someone spit and shook his head.
"Gonna be a chicken joint," he muttered.
"How much chicken can you eat"?

Then we noticed downy feathers
drifting to the sidewalk,
looked up to see a red-tailed hawk
perched under the roof
enjoying its own breakfast,
a fat pigeon whose lifeless body jerked
as the raptor fed.

We stood on that busy street
transfixed by the bloody feast
tongues stilled on this ordinary
morning by so much death
without warning or ceremony,
our hungry mouths open
like the beaks of orphaned baby birds.

Ascension

It wasn't the milk chocolate skin of the girl behind the cash register
that forty years ago might have set our game in motion, skin untouched
by wrinkles, those dry river beds
that mark the flow of passing years.

It wasn't the ancient eyes s wise as Nefertiti's.

It was the way she took my money. When our hands were as close
to touching as they will ever be there was no pull, no tug. I simply
opened my hand and the bill floated skyward through plaster and steel
and roofing shingles, ascending to that place of which all money dreams,
forever free of human striving and desire.

haiku for apocalypse

meteors and fire
pouring down from scarlet skies
there goes the new roof

The Night My Sister Danced with a Mouse

The night my sister danced with a mouse began like an ordinary Sunday evening. My parents were in the kitchen sipping coffee and taking a break from their kids. My sister, Carol, and I were in the living room, polishing off our Swanson Frozen Turkey TV dinners and watching that guy on the Ed Sullivan show spin dinner plates on the end of sticks while the orchestra charged through "The Hungarian Fire Dance." Just as each wobbly plate seemed about to tumble off its stick and crash to Earth, he'd give a little flick with his finger to keep it spinning.

Little did we know that while we sat entranced by Plate Man's battle with gravity, a little brown mouse was creeping across the living room, headed for an epic struggle of its own, a struggle that commenced when Carol glanced down, noticed it tugging at the cuff of her pajama bottom, and levitated (no other verb will do) off the sofa. The startled mouse headed north instead of south, scrabbling up the inside of Carol's pants.

"Aggggh! Get it out! Get it out! Get it out!" she screamed, and tried to evict her uninvited guest with a series of improvised dance steps that had James Brown seen, he would have given up show biz and opened a hardware store. I can't swear her feet ever touched the floor.

When I realized what was happening I fell off the sofa and rolled around on the floor, gasping for air. At the time Carol was thirteen, and four years younger I was a card-carrying member of the Annoying Little Brother's Club.

When our parents ran in from the kitchen to see what the fuss was about, they were greeted by the sight of their daughter, an airborne, wild-eyed dervish, and their son, stretched out on the carpet – flopping like a beached bluefish. The show ended when the mouse finally dropped from Carol's pants and zoomed out of the living room – a near invisible brown blur.

Over the years The Night my Sister Danced with a Mouse became part of our family's personal mythology, a shorthand reminder that we were connected by gravitational fields of laughter and memory in ways we were connected to no one else, that we were not merely four plates spinning off in our separate and solitary dances.

Terror Incognito: A Comedy in Three Acts

Act I: Diagnosis

I can't help noticing the doctor's tie.

It's paisley,
which I usually detest,
but this one's relatively tasteful:
muted-gold paramecia
floating peacefully on a silken lake
of indigo and forest green.
It's a tie I can almost imagine
wearing (if mildly sedated).

The tie is twisted
with the tag facing me. I try to read the label
without being obvious but the lettering's just
a little out of range so I give up and lean back
in the moderately comfortable chair
and as he continues adding
strange new words to my rapidly growing
medical vocabulary I'm listening carefully,
but at the same time I want to tell him
to straighten his tie.
I realize, however, this wouldn't fit
the moment's mood.

On the wall behind him is a framed photograph
of three young children standing in front of a canoe
by a lake, their smiles filled with summer
and the smell of pine.

"Your children," I ask?
"No," he replies, all business.
"I share this office
with another doctor."

Obviously not one for small talk,
he goes on to describe
how the expedition into my brain will proceed;
I start to picture a tiny Lewis and Clark,
striking out in their own canoe to plumb
the virgin territory of my pituitary gland
paddling mightily against rivers of red
resting each night on the banks of
arterial streams, recording their journey
in microscopic notebooks.

Finally, when he leans over to hand me an
"informational pamphlet," his twisted tie
flips around to right itself.

I decide to take this as a good omen.

Act II: The Main Event

The nurse slips the catheter into my arm
and pumps in "a little something to calm me down"
before we head off to the operating room.
When it kicks in as my gurney slides silently
through the hospital labyrinth
I have an excellent view up her nostrils;
I can count the individual hairs.

I enjoy this view for awhile, then my attention
wanders toward the ceiling
and I realize hospital ceilings
are seriously underutilized; just think
how the cost of medical care might be defrayed
if that space was rented for advertising;
while being carted around patients could learn
of all the wonderful goods and services
those of us who survived our operations
would have the opportunity to enjoy.

And while I'm planning the ad campaign
that will revolutionize the health care industry
the clear plastic mask appears and slips
over my face, softly, like a mother's touch
that eases me into the cool and quiet dark.

Act III: After the Show

On this sunny Saturday afternoon in early fall
on my first tentative, unassisted post-surgical outing
Harvard Square is a Fellini movie.
The clown who approaches me
is right out of central casting: striped shirt,
baggy pants with suspenders, bulbous red plastic nose.
Clutching a battered, folded top hat, he says,
"Excuse me sir, would you like to buy a headpiece?
It's overpriced and poorly made."
I glance down. "Yes, very nice, but it
would probably just slip off my bald head."
He pursed his lips. "Have you tried Rogaine?"
"No, not my style. But I've considered Astroturf."
He grins and runs a hand through his polyester Afro.
"Bright green? Like mine?"
"Of course," I reply. I reach for my wallet
and hand him a dollar. "I like your nose."
"I like yours too," he says, then palms the bill.

I continue on my way,
shaking my head at our exchange
when suddenly the sounds and colors
start to swirl around me, tears roll
down surprised cheeks, and I hear
a whispered voice, my own, say again and again:

"You're still here."

A Woman's Laughter

On a recording of the Bill Evans trio,
Live at the Village Vanguard,
late June '61, during a slow, haunting version
of "I Loves You Porgy," at the quietest moment,
in the background, soft but clear,

a woman's laughter.

At first the sound seems jarring, even sacrilegious.
But then again a jazz club's not a concert hall,
listeners in polite rows, knees together,
waiting to cough in the space between movements.
Jazz is cash registers and clinking glasses
and chairs scraping the floor.

And besides it's a pleasant laugh, full of promise.
Easy to see her hand reach out to rest on her
companion's arm. Easy to catch the whiff of lilac or lavender . . .
Always, so many worlds within worlds.

In one world,
A man who follows Evans from gig to gig
sits at the bar alone, transfixed,
ice melting in the forgotten drink.

In one world,
The bartender counts his cash
while dreaming of the waitress's embrace.

In one world,
A woman's laughter.

In one world,
Evans leans over the keys, oblivious to all
but the slow heartbeat bass,
the splash of brushes on cymbal and snare,
fingers poised for what seems like forever
before they settle gently on the final chord.

When a White Boy Plays the Blues

A white boy who plays the blues
for a black audience
is like a brother pulled over
for "Driving While Black,"
an immediate object of suspicion.

When a particular tall, skinny white boy
took the stand on a particular Chicago
summer night in a particular neighborhood club
with cheesy, splintered fake wood paneling
and sputtering neon beer sign
in the window (two of the letters burned out),
in this joint where no fresh-faced logo-covered tourists
lined up outside for a taste of blues Disneyland
the brothers waited with folded arms
to see what he could do.

We didn't care about chops;
any pimply faced first-year
conservatory student can play rings
around Muddy Waters. We were listening
not for notes, but for music.
And if he turned out to be a pretender,
we were looking for clues to identify
the specific nature of the crime.

But when he started playing we were
surprised; the notes that poured from
his guitar and throat weren't dazzling,
but they were true – water from
some well we couldn't find on a map
but we recognized the taste
so we clapped after the first tune
and he glanced at his drummer
with pleasure and relief.

As his set went on, and he got looser,
folks started to clap and grin.
The waitress at the bar
did a little two-step shuffle while she waited
for her drinks; some guy with a gold tooth
played percussion on a beer bottle with a set of keys.

The verdict was in. It was clear we all belonged in this place,
on this hot night, with our cold beers, that we were all
in our own ways outsiders, together,
faces pressed to the glass of the American Dream.

Prayer

In a quiet corner of the supermarket parking lot
an employee in red t-shirt
kneels on a piece of cardboard,
bows, then rises to speak the holy words,
his view of Mecca unimpeded
by the dumpster and unpainted wooden fence.

When Grief Comes Calling

Grief waits patiently for the phone to ring
to bring the midnight news that can't be borne,
but must be borne. Grief comes quietly
to the door, slips through the keyhole
like smoke, or the long tail of a bad dream
that wraps around you and won't let go.

When grief comes calling
try as you might you cannot bar
this uninvited guest who sours the milk,
turns each bite of food to sand and dust.

But as time passes, small pleasures begin their
slow, tip-toed return – the sound of dry leaves
dancing on the wind, or the smell of baking bread.

And then one night as you drive
over the crest of a hill a full moon,
lying low and huge in the sky, leaps into view
like a giant child playing hide and seek,
and in that moment of surprise and wonder
you cross the border of a new land
where grief still resides, but no longer rules.

Memento Mori

I
According to legend a Roman general
who won a great battle would be paraded
through the city,
standing in a chariot, waving to the tens
of thousands lining the boulevard
cheering and shouting his name.
Behind him would stand a common soldier,
or sometimes a slave, holding a crown
above the general's head in a
gently mocking gesture and whispering in his ear,
to keep his vanity and pride in check,
"Remember . . . you must die."

II
There's a tiny bump on the back
of my right hand, invisible to the eye.
Years ago when I was being prepped
for brain surgery, a catheter
was inserted there and the bump remains.

Sometimes when I'm tired, or bored
or anxious, I'll realize
my finger has been moving over
it slowly, back and forth,
stroking it like a talisman,
a reminder to make the most
of the never-to-be-repeated day.

III
The late afternoon light that
slants through the blinds
painting zebra stripes
on the dining room table
takes me back to my sister's last day
when she lay in the hospital bed
and the sunlight streaming through the window
illuminated the salt-and-pepper hair
wispy and dry, spread out against her pillow.

Dreamtime

The tribesman standing on the Redline train
dressed in breechcloth only, body covered
with red and yellow paint, seems a long way from home,
and by "home" I mean not only the sun-seared
Australian landscape, but a long way from his time.

Yet I'm the one worried about time; to him
The idea of time means nothing. His people live
In the Dreamtime, where yesterday, today, tomorrow
Are but drops of water in a river without beginning or end.
It's the quantum physics of the outback, a wisdom that was
Ancient thousands of years before the pyramids were born.

It's a wisdom I find hard to appreciate on a rainy Tuesday morning
Before my second cup of coffee. I know, without knowing how
I know, that his presence is meant for me. No one else
can see him. The other passengers' ordinary faces are all
lit by the glow of their plastic toys.

Whatever message he carries for me, I don't want.
So I make a point of not meeting his eyes. I needn't bother;
He's not looking at me, or at anyone else on the train.
He's simply standing as the stations slip by
like beads on a prayer rope, and when I get off at Harvard Square
he doesn't acknowledge me in any way, just maintains
his silent vigil as the trains shoots down the dark tunnel.

But something has shifted, some portal cracked open.
Suddenly on the platform I see myself in first grade
at the little wooden desk, in clip-on tie
proudly clutching a newly sharpened pencil.
That image fades, and now I'm the young man about town,
admiring my reflection in a shop window as I pass,
hair-covered head empty as a paper cup.

That image fades, and now I'm watching my mother
being lowered into the ground.

That image fades, and now I see my eyes stare
out of a face lined with wrinkles. A finger beckons me near
I take one reluctant step forward, then another,
and softly, in a voice filled with dust,
he begins to speak.

A Conversation with My Younger Self

Congratulations to you, newly hatched grownup
in first solo apartment, boxes scattered
about like soldiers exhausted after a long march,
King Kong poster taped to the wall,
a little crooked, now guarding the kitchen.

The friends who helped you move are long gone,
empty beer bottles and pizza boxes all that remain.
Of course, hooking up the stereo
was your first priority and now Jimi Hendrix roars
through these little rooms like a low-flying fighter jet.

I peer at you through time's gauze curtain
and realize how much I want to say. I want
to tell you to go outside and look at the stars,
because sometimes it's good to feel small.

I want to tell you a woman's love is a precious thing,
not just a Saturday night's entertainment.

I want to tell you to turn down the stereo and call your mother.

I want to tell you all this and so much more,
but you can't hear a word I say, because this isn't
a conversation; it's the world's oldest bad joke,
and I'm the punch line, this white-haired ghost
brimming with after-the-fact wisdom, on a boat
pulling away from shore, sliding through dark water
to some destination unknown, hopping up and down

on one leg to get your attention, waving my arms
and shouting, as if what I'm saying
might actually make a difference.

And maybe you glance up for a moment
puzzled by some disturbance in the air
as you eat one last slice of cold pizza
off some dead grandmother's thrift shop dinner plate.

NEW AND SELECTED WORKS

Every New Thing
for Ann

Every new thing is an act of treason,
a betrayal of the comfortable, the familiar.
An animal that has known only the cage
will cringe in the corner if the door
suddenly swings open, squealing on
ancient, rusted hinges.
If I have one wish for you, for me,
for us all, it's to remember that our own cages
are locked only by the fear of change,
that we have the power to shove those doors open
to take one step, then another,
into a new world.

Purgatory Road – Charles Coe

"I believe that what people call God is something in all of us. I believe that what Jesus and Mohammed and Buddha and all the rest said was right. It's just that the translations have gone wrong." – *John Lennon*

Some poems in this collection have appeared in *Ibbetson Street Press*, *Meat for Tea*, *Multiplicity Magazine*, and *The Red Letter*.

Charles Coe

PURGATORY
ROAD

POEMS

haiku for a new season

when will it be time
for all the ancient angers
to melt like spring snow

Opportunity

A woman in the park stands talking to a friend
while a little girl sitting behind her on a bench
feeds an ice cream cone to the family dog.

Dogs are noted opportunists where food is concerned,
and this one's no exception, making short work
of the job at hand (or rather, the job at tongue)
while the woman's attention is elsewhere.

Funny how our idea of what's important
changes with time. When I am older and grayer
looking back on this day, I won't remember
the headlines, the daily litany of atrocities and disasters.
I won't remember the comings and goings
of some flavor-of-the month celebrity.

I'll remember the way the wind tossed
dry leaves on a sunny autumn afternoon.
I'll remember a dog's tongue,
resolute and efficient,
and a little girl's conspiratorial smile.

Snapshots from Cuba

I
In Havana on a tourist bus, plush, comfortable seats,
air conditioning, a cooler in back filled with ice, bottled water,
and apple juice, snacks in a bag behind the driver's seat.

While we're stopped at a light next to a crowded city bus,
I meet the eyes of a man standing, hanging from a strap,
body sagging with the weight of a day's work,
rough clothes covered with dust and dirt.

We are separated by two layers of glass, and a slice of hot,
humid air, three feet and a million miles apart.

II
A young boy alone, kicking a soccer ball in a dirt yard,
two boxes against a fence for a makeshift goal,
moving to silent salsa.

III
Three men, two locals and a tourist, sharing a drink,
surrounded by cats wandering the plaza.
Tourist says, "When I was here in '92
I don't remember seeing so many cats."

The locals exchange a glance. One says,

"Well...things are better now..."

Scenes from a Vanished City

The teenaged boys who hung out in front
of the pinball arcade, smoking cigarette after cigarette
under the suspicious gaze of the cop on the beat.

The old black man in what's now a real estate office
who dished out ribs and fried chicken and collard greens
and mac and cheese to drunken revelers pouring
from parties and clubs at closing time.

The little storefront coffee houses,
where earnest young people sang and strummed
odes to the world they dreamed of creating.

The windows of skyscrapers that glowed
like burnished gold in the late afternoon light
as you passed in the elevated train.

The young black man in the ancient
heavy coat he wore in weather fair or
foul who sat on the steps of a boarded-up
brownstone, now a multi-million-dollar property,
and never spoke, just stared into a future
only he could see.

I Wish I'd Held My Father's Hand

My father put what he wanted to buy on the drugstore counter and said a polite "Good Afternoon" to the young white clerk, who didn't return the greeting or meet his eye, just stared at the items as if Father had dumped a bucket of kitchen scraps, and then with exquisite slowness that dripped contempt, began to ring them up.

It was an ordinary day in Indiana in the early sixties. Everywhere a black man went he had to bite his tongue. Looking back over the years, I wish I could go back to that afternoon when my father stood quiet and still while that punk tried to put him in his place. I wish I could have caught his eye, delivered the silent message that I understood what he had to go through every day to keep the peace, to raise his family.

I wish I'd held my father's hand.

Elegy

A dead baby deer is lying by the side of the highway,
a flash of white and brown I notice
in a fleeting moment of surprise and dismay.

We all have seen possums and squirrels
and raccoons and whatnot
killed on roads and highways,
but I have never seen a deer, and I'm
flooded with unanswerable questions:
did it wander away from its mother?
Was it orphaned and stumbled in confusion
onto this highway for its first and final
encounter with the world of humans?

Did someone pull onto the shoulder,
drag it to the side of road, take out
a phone and with shaking fingers
punch in the numbers to inform whatever
earthly authorities oversee such matters?

I speed along in my two-thousand-pound chunk
of metal, captured by the irrational thought
that there was something I might have done,
or could do now.

But I have nothing to offer, nothing to add.
Can only think of deep forests that will go
unexplored, and tender green leaves untasted.

Butt Dialing Jesus

There was a time when voices emanating from my pants
would have caused concern. But now I simply shrugged
and pulled out my phone to hear a recording:
"You have reached The Son of God.
I am currently speaking with another supplicant.
But please hold; your salvation is important to me."

This was followed by music.
I expected celestial choirs, or maybe an elevator-friendly
version of "My Sweet Lord," but was instead treated
to acoustic Delta blues guitar, interrupted after
a few minutes by the voice of Himself, greeting me
by name and asking how he could serve.

I was startled. Didn't expect to actually get through.
"Umm...what's the one true religion?" I asked,
flustered, just to have something to say.
"All of them," he replied. "None of them."

I was taken aback. "What? That's it?"
"That's it," he said. "Follow the Golden Rule.
Leave the campground cleaner than you found it.
Anything else? I have a lot of people on hold."
I had nothing, and mumbled my thanks.

He said "Go in Peace" and broke the connection.
I put down the phone and stared out the window.
The guy across the street was clearing snow
off his sidewalk. Never really liked that dude,
but I grabbed my shovel to go lend a hand.

Incantations

Late one night our family was driving home, Father at the wheel, Mother dozing beside him, head against the window, our enormous Ford station wagon humming along, a ship sailing the asphalt ocean. When "PT 109" as I think of it now wasn't full of tools, Father let my sister Carol and me pop down the back seat, spread a pile of blankets and stretch out, drifting off sometimes, lulled by the vibrations of road.

The radio was on and there was a sudden crackle and hum as the station Father had tuned in gave way to a disembodied voice reciting the results of high school football games from some far away state. The seemingly endless recitation of unfamiliar places took on a hypnotic quality, an incantation like the Latin words, meaningless to me, the priest spoke at Mass as I kneeled on the altar in cassock and surplus, waiting my cue to pour water over his fingers and hand him a towel to dry them before he gave communion.

I didn't understand how this was happening. I didn't know that at night AM radio signals can travel hundreds of miles by reflecting off the ionosphere, bouncing back to Earth, and being picked up on radios impossibly far away. I didn't know this phenomenon, "skywave," it's called, happens only at night, because the ionosphere doesn't reflect radio waves when warmed by the sun.

I didn't know the science, it seemed to me we'd just slipped somehow through a portal to another universe. As that spectral voice droned on I lay in back of the station wagon, mesmerized by the endless stream of numbers that symbolized the joys and disappointments of young gladiators who'd fought their epic battles under the lights, before families and friends, on grass-covered fields, in little faraway towns I would never know.

Capistrano

A man in a torn, dirty overcoat
paces the sidewalk
in front of the coffee shop
slowly, back and forth
head down, talking to himself.
He's here often. Sometimes
he'll come in, sit awhile
have a conversation with the air,
then hop up and wander back outside
to continue his vigil.

Why does this place of all places
call him? What draws him here
again and again and again
like the birds who return each year
to fill the California sky?

Quality of Attention

I'm at the kitchen sink washing dishes
and see through the window a little brown
rabbit making its way through the yard next door
ears and nose twitching, alert for predators.

As quietly as possible I lift the screen for a better look
but the rabbit freezes at the faint sound,
suddenly no longer flesh and blood,
but a stone garden statue sitting under
a chrysanthemum bush.
After a vigilant moment during which
I'm silent and still, it starts to move again,
nibbling and poking through the grass.

I'm humbled by this creature's quality of attention.
When I *think* I'm concentrating,
my mind is actually a leaky garden hose:
(My nose itches. Am I ready for that meeting?
Who's frying onions?)

I rinse a plate and put it on the dish rack.
When I look up again the rabbit is gone.

Beasts of Burden

Item from the "Cape Ann Light and Gloucester Telegraph," March 8, 1873: *"A block of granite was hauled to the Rockport railroad station on Wednesday that required thirteen yoke of oxen to get it through the streets."*

Curious people line either side of the dusty road, mesmerized by the slow procession, oxen pulling a massive wagon that creaks and groans under its load, an ancient and eternal slab, formed when the world was young, that will outlast onlookers by a hundred generations.

It would be a foolish to think these animals understand their role in history, that they know their load will grace some grand edifice of the young republic. They are simply beasts of burden who pull when prodded, eat when fed.

But millennia ago, long before human masters with yokes and whips, their ancestors freely roamed the endless plains. Now at night, lying asleep in barns, do they ever stir at the touch of some distant memory, some timeless dream of fragrant, waving grass stretching beyond the horizon?

Fish Story

At the supermarket with dinner company coming,
in something of a hurry.

I'm standing at the fish counter while the person
ahead of me is in the middle of a private piscine
consultation, asking whether to choose this fish
or that fish or this fish for a particular dish,
inquiring into the provenance of the finalists,
asking for cooking advice

and I realize this errand will not be a quick one
after all, that I will indeed be standing at this
fish counter until, no beyond the end of time
when the human race has long since vanished,
a fading image on the retina of the universe
and the Earth itself but a lifeless cinder
drifting in eternal circles around the sun.

Purgatory Road

We were told in Parochial school that Purgatory was the place for souls not damned to Hell, but needing purification before ascending to Heaven, souls guilty of unconfessed venial, not mortal sins. There was fire and suffering in Purgatory, but just for awhile. How long a while was not explained. But we were told that if you died before you confessed your venial sins the chances would pretty good you'd wind up in Purgatory.

Purgatory wasn't like Hell where the damned burned for all eternity. As grade school kids, the concept of eternity was somewhat unclear. But one day Sister Helen explained eternity by telling us to imagine a solid brass globe, the size of the Earth. Once every thousand years, a dove flies by and brushes the globe with the tip of a wing. The time it would take that touch to wear the brass globe to nothing is just the first second of eternity. Sister Helen scanned our small, perplexed brown faces and nodded, confident her explanation had gotten her point across.

My main takeaway was that that even if Purgatory was a drag, it was better than Hell. At least you eventually got sprung. I thought of Purgatory as Heaven's Waiting Room, like the doctor's office, tables piled with ancient copies of "Reader's Digest" and "Life Magazine" and "Highlights for Children." Only with fire. Of course, I wasn't foolish enough to share any of these speculations with the nuns or priests. We weren't allowed to question matters of theology.

The rites and rituals of youth, the mysterious incantations in a secret and ancient language, the calm, inflexible certainties of the Baltimore Catechism, the dark and quiet confessional box, are all dust-covered relics in my mind's closet. But one time, driving through a small New England town I passed a sign for "Purgatory Road," and the name tossed me into the Wayback Machine, to when my life was ruled by pale faces draped in black, who spoke with great assurance in the voice of God on all matters spiritual.

I think now that maybe this earthbound life is itself something like a Purgatory Road, that navigating the potholes of our sorrows and disappointments, the roadblocks of fear and failure, the endless random acts of casual cruelty, is our own rite of purification, that crucible of cold fire through which we all must pass to become ourselves.

Something on the Wind

A car waiting at the red light has a dog
with head stuck out the back window,
tongue hanging, snout twitching, beguiled
by some intriguing smell. The average dog nose
is a million times more sensitive than a human's,
a bloodhound's nose, a hundred million times.

This dog's a mutt, not a bloodhound,
genetic fruit salad, a United Nations of Dog,
but it has a fine nose, and appears
unconcerned about its lack of pedigree,
focused instead on whatever it's sniffing,
and it occurs to me there might not be
a more contented creature on the planet
than a dog with head stuck out a car window.

The light turns green, the dog moves on to new
olfactory adventures, and I wonder what it
smelled here, what it smelled that
I could never detect with this feeble
human nose, even if that nose
weren't covered by this mask I'm hoping
will protect me from something on the wind.

Communion: Spring, 2020

Do you remember those times we'd all meet
at some favorite restaurant? Stepping in
from the cold, breathing clouds of garlic,
shrugging off coats for the welcoming hugs?

We'd examine the menu with the care
of archeologists blowing dust off a
newly discovered Sanskrit tablet. And we'd sit
so close, touching sometimes, passing platters
back and forth, everyone yakking at once,
pausing to join in a ragged chorus of
"Happy Birthday" drifting over from a nearby table.

And finally, as our ravaged plates made
their way back to the kitchen, sometimes
we'd pose for a picture taken on someone's
phone by an indulgent server, arms
wrapped around each other, grinning
like high school kids at graduation.

Now those of us who live alone
search cookbooks and computers
for the dishes we make for one,
post pictures of our creations online,
not to brag, but to share communion
the only way we can.

Secret Chord
for Leonard Cohen

They all thought this little shepherd boy was a fool to face Goliath.
In truth I thought something of the same myself, tossing and sweating
on my bed of straw the night before that fateful day, visited by visions
of the giant's sword, long as I was tall, cleaving enemies from shoulder
to waist with but a single blow.

When I made music for Saul, my King, to soothe his troubled soul,
it did not anger me that he so feared the giant he had me do battle in his
stead. It was not my place to judge, but simply play my harp to ease his mind.

He would send his servants away so it was just the two of us,
the sound of my harp echoing through that spacious, ornate, empty
room, while he stared into the distance at something only he could see.

Now so many years later as this crown sits heavy on my own head,
I feel the burden of the throne. We who would be the kings or queens
of our own realms seldom realize how difficult it truly is to rule oneself,
seldom realize how quickly the years fly, all the words said or left unsaid,
all the golden moments that each of us lets drift to earth,
until in the end, one can become a master of regret.

Saul, my King, what do I say to you now across this gulf of years?
Do I say,
"Offer up your sadness, your fear, your failures, your weakness, your
longings.
Offer them up, offer up this song of your true self, to the one
who accepts it without judgment?

Who can know, can ever know, what secret music flows
like precious blood through the chambers of the human heart?

Just Another Day
for Juneteenth

On the first day of the New Year, 1863, on a Texas plantation, a man opens his eyes as sunlight streams through the windows of his little shack. The windows aren't really windows, just holes in the walls covered with tarpaper when the cold winds blow.

This man rises from his rough bed of hay, splashes water on his face, and eats a breakfast of cold fatback and cornbread. It's winter time, too early to harvest sugar cane, work the press that rolls stalks flat to extract the juice, the press that longs to crush careless fingers. It's too early to stir the giant iron pots that splash boiling cane juice on your skin. January is too early to plant, or pick, or haul, or bale cotton. Those hot and thankless days will come soon enough. Today's a day to build stalls in the master's stable.

When this man steps out of his shack into the morning light, his woman is already gone. Up at the big house, nursing the mistress's baby, and after that will churn butter, and after that will sit with needle and thread, to mend a rip in the master's shirt, and after that will kill and pluck and gut a chicken, and after that will haul in wood and stoke the stove, and after that will weed the garden, and after that will go outside to stir a cauldron of lye soap, and after that will once again nurse the baby while her mistress sits on the porch, in the shade, sipping cool tea and reading passages from her Bible.

On this first day of the New Year, two thousand miles to the north and east a tall, bearded white man sits at a desk, pauses a moment, as if awaiting guidance, dips his pen in ink, and writes the words, all persons held as slaves" within the rebellious states "are, and henceforward shall be free."

As his pen scratches slowly across the page, two thousand miles to the south and west, a man and a woman toil beneath the Texas sun. For them, it's just another day.

Two years later another bearded white man will sit astride his horse in Galveston and read General Orders No. 3: "The people of Texas are informed that, in accordance with a proclamation from the Executive of the United States, all slaves are free." Maybe the man and woman who built stalls in a stable and nursed their masters' baby on the day Abraham Lincoln wrote the Emancipation Proclamation are still alive when those words spread like wildfire through the state of Texas. Or maybe they are not.

However you pray, whether you put your hands together to speak Holy Words, lower your head for a moment of silence, or simply lift a glass, take a moment to remember those enslaved women and men who lived out their lives never knowing they were now free, no longer chattel, never knowing they were no longer merely beasts of burden, subject to the whims and whips of overseers.

For the Africans on Slave Ships Who Committed Suicide By Jumping Overboard

You had to plan carefully, wait for the moment
when a deck hand or first mate's attention was elsewhere
before climbing quickly onto the railing
to dive into the dark waters.

Sometimes a few of you joined hands,
gazed into each other's eyes a moment before leaping.

After suicides ship's officers would mourn.
Each death reduced the journey's profit.

Some of you believed you would rise from the sea
find yourselves at home in your villages once again,
walking down the hills where you played as children,
toward the smell of roasting yams and the sound
of crowing roosters, loved ones celebrating your return
as the morning sun licked salt water from your ebony skin.

Flight, Interrupted

Late night at a subway station. I'm the only one getting off, no one's getting on, and I stand a long moment watching the train disappear down the tunnel.

A solitary pigeon has somehow managed to navigate three levels from the street down to the platform and is walking back and forth along the tiles, cooing, head bobbing. As I walk toward the escalator it flies up to the ceiling, spooked by my nearness, flutters along the solid barrier, and finding no path to familiar sky returns to pace the platform, a little farther down.

I make my way to the escalator looking for an employee to tell but there's nobody there, never anybody there at night anymore, and as I reach the street and step into the cool air my poet brain instantly chugs into motion, the machinery of metaphor rattles and cranks, hissing steam and spitting images as I consider the bird's plight. Maybe Freud would have said, this isn't a metaphor. It's pigeon. A living, breathing creature with a beating heart like mine, trapped in a place it neither belongs nor understands.

But the seed of a poem has already taken root. I'm already comparing the pigeon's dilemma to every creature constrained and bewildered by whatever invisible ceilings keep us from taking wing.

in the days to come

in the days to come
when i have gone
to wherever i am going
sometimes when you
walk along the shore
stop for a moment
bare toes in warm sand
gaze at the rainbow sky
and i'll be there
the salt spray
kissing your cheek

CHARLES COE

Charles Coe is the author of four books of poetry: *Purgatory Road, All Sins Forgiven: Poems for my Parents, Picnic on the Moon,* and *Memento Mori,* all published by Leapfrog Press. He is also the author of *Spin Cycles,* a novella published by Gemma Media. Charles was selected as a Boston Literary Light by the Associates of the Boston Public Library and is a former artist fellow at the St. Botolph Club in Boston. A short film by filmmaker Roberto Mighty, "Peach Pie," that was based on his poem, "Fortress", has been shown at film festivals nationwide. Another short film, "Charles Coe: Man of Letters," also by Roberto Mighty was named "Outstanding Documentary Short" at the 2020 Roxbury Film Festival. His poems have been set by composers Kitty Brazelton, Beth Denisch, Paul Frucht, and Robert Moran.

Charles was a 2017 artist-in-residence for the city of Boston, where he created an oral history project focused on residents of Mission Hill. He is poetry editor of "Multiplicity," an online literary journal published by Bay Path University in Longmeadow, Massachusetts, and associate editor of "About Place," an online literary journal published by Black Earth Institute.

Charles has served as poet-in-residence at Wheaton College, the Newton Public Schools, and at the Chautauqua Institution in New York State. He is an adjunct professor of English at Salve Regina University in Newport, Rhode Island, and Bay Path University, in Longmeadow, Massachusetts, where he teaches in both MFA programs. He serves on the Steering Committee of the Boston Chapter of The National Writers Union, a labor union for free-lance writers and editors. He is also on the Board of Directors of The New England Poetry Club and Revolutionary Spaces, Inc., the organization that manages and programs activities at Boston's Old South Meeting House and the Old State House, site of the Boston Massacre.

www.ingramcontent.com/pod-product-compliance
Lightning Source LLC
Jackson TN
JSHW080735140125
77033JS00038B/412